How to Catapult a Castle

Machines That Brought Down the Battlements

James de Winter

Capstone
press®

Mankato, Minnesota

Fact Finders is published by Capstone Press,
a Capstone Publishers company.
151 Good Counsel Drive, P.O. Box 669,
Mankato, Minnesota 56002.
www.capstonepress.com

First published 2008
Copyright © 2008 A & C Black Publishers Limited

Produced for A & C Black by
MONKEY PUZZLE MEDIA Ltd
Monkey Puzzle Media Ltd
The Rectory, Eyke, Woodbridge
Suffolk IP12 2QW, UK

Library of Congress Cataloging-in-Publication Data

Winter, James de.
  How to catapult a castle: machines that brought down
  the battlements / by James de Winter.
  p. cm. -- (Fact finders. extreme!)
  Includes bibliographical references and index.
  Summary: "Presents the science behind building and
  defending castles including the use of simple machines,
  such as pulleys and levers"--Provided by publisher.
  ISBN-13: 978-1-4296-3118-1 (hardcover)
  ISBN-10: 1-4296-3118-X (hardcover)
  ISBN-13: 978-1-4296-3138-9 (pbk.)
  ISBN-10: 1-4296-3138-4 (pbk.)
  1. Siege warfare<Juvenile literature. I. Title. II. Series.

UG444.W56 2009
623.4'41--dc22

2008023568

Editor: Cath Senker
Design: Mayer Media Ltd
Picture research: Lynda Lines
Series consultant: Jane Turner

This book is produced using paper that is made from
wood grown in managed, sustainable forests. It is natural,
renewable, and recyclable. The logging and manufacturing
processes conform to the environmental regulations of
the country of origin.

Printed in China by C & C Offset Printing Co., Ltd

Picture acknowledgements
akg-images p. 13 (British Library); Alamy pp. 10 top
(Malcolm Fairman), 16 (Ian Goodrick), 21 (Holmes
Garden Photos), 23 (Jeff Morgan Heritage), 26 (The Print
Collector), 29 top (PCL), 29 bottom (Wendy Connett);
Art Archive pp. 9 (Real Biblioteca de lo Escorial/Gianni
Dagli Orti), 18 (Alfredo Dagli Orti); Bridgeman Art
Library pp. 7 (Kunsthistorisches Museum, Vienna, Austria),
17 (Private Collection/© Look and Learn); Corbis p. 15
(Chris Hellier); Getty Images pp. 11 (Geoff Dann), 14
(Travel Ink), 24 top (Bridgeman Art Library), 28 (Dallas
Stribley); iStockphoto pp. 5 (Mike Modine), 12 (S. Greg
Panosian); Kobal Collection p. 19 (Morgan Creek/
Warner Bros); MPM Images p. 10 bottom;
Photolibrary.com p. 6 (Phototake Science/Carol and Mike
Werner); Topfoto.co.uk p. 27 (The Royal Armouries/HIP);
Twentieth Century Fox pp. 1, 20, 24 bottom; Warwick
Castle p. 25; Wikimedia Commons pp. 4, 8, 22.

The front cover shows a reconstruction of the battle
between Saracens and Christians for control of Jerusalem
in 1187 (Twentieth Century Fox).

Every effort has been made to contact copyright holders
of material reproduced in this book. Any omissions will be
rectified in subsequent printings if notice is given to the
publishers.

CONTENTS

Abbreviations m stands for meters • ft stands for feet • in stands for inches • cm stands for centimeters • km stands for kilometers

Castles—from wood to stone

Back in the Middle Ages, rich and important people had massive houses to themselves. This was fine for them—until other people decided to raid their home and steal their things. This happened quite often, so wealthy people made their houses stronger to resist attack. Their homes became castles.

It started with wood

The first castles in Europe were built about 1,000 years ago. Early castles were made from wood.

Wood is good to build with, but it burns easily. To break into a castle, raiders simply had to set fire to it, stand back, and watch their enemies run for their lives. From around A.D.1100, people in Europe began to build castles from stone instead.

This wooden castle in Biskupin, Poland, is on top of a hill. It is a good place to be safe from attack.

Middle Ages the time between the 5th and 15th centuries

The castle is protected by rings of stone and by water.

Caerphilly Castle in Wales was built more than 1,000 years ago. Parts of it are still standing today.

The giant lake around the castle was dug by hand.

You can't burn this castle down—it's made of stone.

The lake around the castle made it hard for attackers to approach

Building a castle

In the Middle Ages, it took at least a decade to build a castle, and it cost a fortune. Hundreds of workers were brought on to the job. Luckily, simple machines such as wheels and pulleys made their work much easier.

By using a pulley, you can lift a weight that is much heavier than you are. Modern pulleys are similar to the ones that were used to build castles.

Pulling your weight

The more pulley wheels there are, the more you can lift. With three pulley wheels, you can lift three times more than you could with just one rope.

A modern pulley, used to lift a small boat.

machine a piece of equipment with moving parts that does a particular job

1 The rope attached to the wheel lifts a heavy object.

2 The men inside the **treadwheel** walk forward. It's easier to walk than lift.

3 The treadwheel changes the direction of the force from along . . .

4 . . . to up.

treadwheel large wheel with a rope attached for lifting heavy objects

7

Keeping the enemy out

It was great to have a strong castle, but sometimes people did need to get in and out. Most castles had only one main entrance, which made it easier to guard. Some had a **moat** around them. Only the bravest attackers would dare to cross.

Castles all over the world had moats. Matsumoto Castle is in Japan. This castle has a secret level with no windows. Food and weapons were stored here.

Moats were often filled by linking them to nearby rivers or streams. Chillon Castle in Geneva, Switzerland, was built on an island at the edge of Lake Geneva. That way, there was no need to build a moat.

Watch out!

Large spikes were sometimes hidden underwater to spear any enemies who tried to swim across.

moat a huge ditch around a castle, usually filled with water

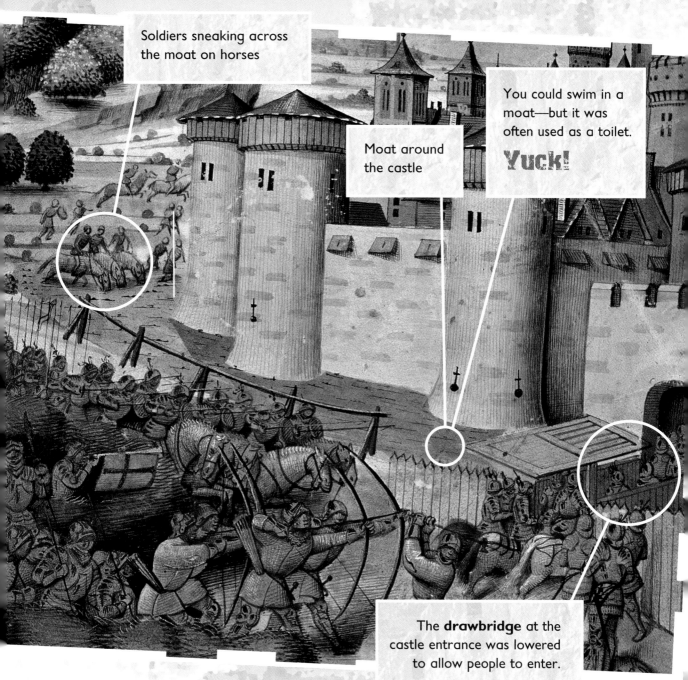

Soldiers sneaking across the moat on horses

Moat around the castle

You could swim in a moat—but it was often used as a toilet.

Yuck!

The **drawbridge** at the castle entrance was lowered to allow people to enter.

Soldiers fighting outside a medieval French castle.

drawbridge bridge that can be raised and lowered to open and close the castle entrance

The spiked gate

Even if you crossed the moat and got over the drawbridge, you would come up against the **portcullis. This spiked gate made of wood and metal helped to keep out unwanted visitors.**

Once you were past the moat, drawbridge, and portcullis, you'd still have to pass under the **murder holes**. These were holes in the roof along the main way into the castle.

The defenders used the murder holes to drop dangerous things on invading solders to kill or injure them. They dropped boiling water, hot sand, or red-hot stones.

A caltrop has four spikes. Wherever it lands, one spike always points upward. Ouch!

Caltrops

The Romans used **caltrops** over 2,000 years ago. They dropped them in front of the charging enemy to spike their feet. The same idea is used in barbed-wire fences.

The downward force would be enough to skewer many people.

It took many men to lift up the portcullis.

When the portcullis was released, **gravity** rapidly pulled it down.

You wouldn't want to hang around under a portcullis!

gravity the force that pulls all things downward

Ladders and siege towers

The overhanging walls of Bodiam Castle in Sussex made it hard to climb up.

If it wasn't possible to break into a castle through the portcullis, another way was over the wall. Many castles were built with **machicolations**—overhanging walls that made it tricky to climb up.

Don't look up

To make it even harder for invaders, there were holes in the overhanging parts. The defenders dropped heavy objects and boiling liquids on to their enemies.

machicolation   the overhanging part of the wall at the top of a castle

Soldiers using a siege tower to attack a castle.

A **siege tower** was a tall tower with ladders on the inside and shields on the outside. It helped attacking soldiers to get close to the castle walls.

The flap is like a mini-drawbridge. It is lowered to let the soldiers in and out.

The soldiers are protected inside the siege tower until it is time to go into action.

Wheels make it easy to move the tower into place.

Battering rams

If you couldn't get over the walls, you could try to smash them down. This was tricky to do with your bare hands but easier if you had a battering ram.

The battering ram was often a big tree trunk on wheels. Strong men pushed it against a weak part of the castle wall.

The walls of this castle in Leicestershire, England, were thicker at the bottom than at the top. This made them hard to knock down.

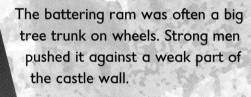

Aiming low

Battering rams were usually aimed low. If you knocked a hole at the bottom of the wall, it was likely the whole wall would fall down.

A huge medieval battering ram in France.

The triangular shield protected the soldiers while they tried to knock down the castle wall.

Falling objects rolled safely to the sides.

All the energy from the men and moving log was focused on the end of the battering ram. This helped to break down the wall.

This battering ram has a wooden end but some had a metal end.

tering ram large pole used to smash down castle walls

Tunneling under and burning pigs

If you couldn't get over or through the walls, the next plan was to dig underneath—very sneaky! Using some spades and wood, and plenty of soldiers to dig deep, you could topple an entire castle wall.

THE DAILY SIEGE

1215

FORTY BURNING PIGS AND THE WALLS COME TUMBLING DOWN

In an amazing scene in Kent last night, the air was filled with a mix of sizzling bacon and dust from a collapsing castle.

"Crazy" King John was so desperate to return to Rochester Castle that he was prepared to try anything.

He filled tunnels under the castle with

After the massive fire, the castle was rebuilt.

pig fat, started a fire and stood well back. The flaming fat burned the supports holding up the tunnel and castle, and within hours the walls came tumbling down.

Medieval burglar alarm

Soldiers in the castle placed bowls of water on the floor to detect tunneling below. If they saw ripples in the water, they knew people were digging underneath.

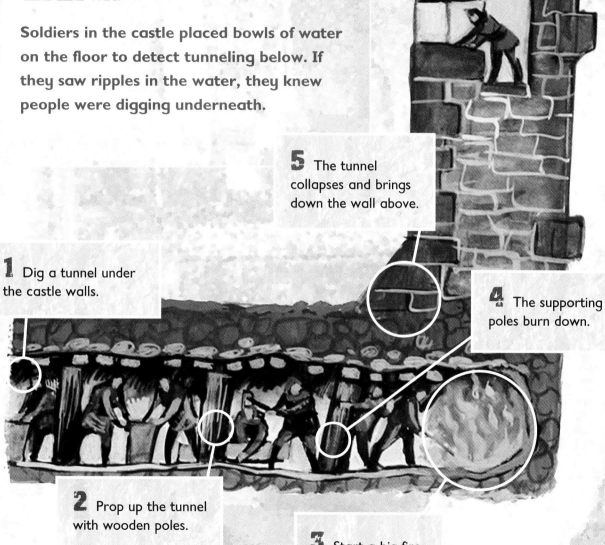

5 The tunnel collapses and brings down the wall above.

1 Dig a tunnel under the castle walls.

4 The supporting poles burn down.

2 Prop up the tunnel with wooden poles.

3 Start a big fire inside the tunnel.

Longbows and flaming arrows

If you had given up on getting inside the castle, the next best thing was to try to kill everyone inside. With most of them dead, it would be easier to get in. With a longbow, you could fire arrows into the castle from a long way away.

*You can see the **battlements** along the top of this medieval castle in Italy.*

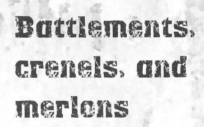

Battlements, crenels, and merlons

Castle walls were built with battlements. Archers fired on attackers through narrow slits called **crenels**. While shooting, they hid behind the **merlons** (the solid parts) to protect themselves.

battlements narrow wall along the top of the castle wall to protect the castle's defenders

18

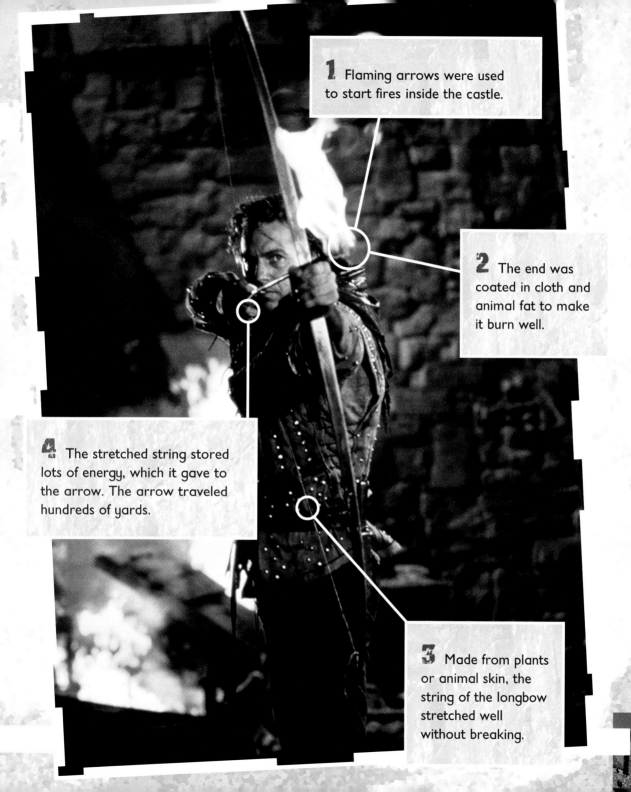

1 Flaming arrows were used to start fires inside the castle.

2 The end was coated in cloth and animal fat to make it burn well.

4 The stretched string stored lots of energy, which it gave to the arrow. The arrow traveled hundreds of yards.

3 Made from plants or animal skin, the string of the longbow stretched well without breaking.

Deadly crossbows

Longbows were very powerful, but the crossbow could be a more deadly weapon in attack. The arrows—called bolts—were shorter but usually heavier and could be fired faster.

A **ballista** used in a reconstruction of the defense of Jerusalem by Christian forces in 1187.

The bigger the crossbow, the greater the damage it could do. The ballista was a giant crossbow in a frame. It was even more deadly than the handheld one.

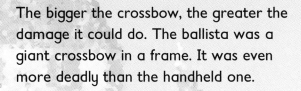

With more energy stored, the bolt travels **farther** and **faster**

The energy to fire the bolt is stored in stretched or twisted twine.

The twine was made from a tough fiber that would not fray.

Some crossbows used levers or cogs to pull back the twine and make it very tight.

The crossbow is fired with a trigger.

How to catapult a castle!

A catapult is not just a weapon. Nowadays you can ride in a giant catapult where you are the missile!

A small catapult called a slingshot can fire stones. A large one can fire huge missiles. **In the Middle Ages, invading soldiers used giant catapults called mangonels to catapult castles and send the walls crashing down.**

In a bungee, the ropes form the catapult. The energy stored in the **stretched** rubber shifts to you when you let go. The more the rubber stretches, the more energy is released, and the faster and higher you go!

Grapes you cannot eat

Sometimes soldiers filled the spoon of the mangonel with lots of little rocks to spread the damage over a wide area. This was called grapeshot.

This mangonel stands on the ground. Some had wheels so they could be moved easily.

In battle, a normal catapult couldn't fire objects far enough, and so the mangonel was developed. The missile was placed in a giant spoon inside a frame.

The mangonel was good for firing missiles fast and low to smash castle walls.

The energy for firing is stored in twisted ropes.

missile any object thrown or fired toward a target

Seesaw powered: the trebuchet

Have you ever jumped down on one end of a seesaw and seen the other end shoot up? Then you already have a good idea of how a trebuchet works.

Rather than stretching rope or strings, the trebuchet stores energy in a very heavy object that has been lifted up.

The trebuchet could fire missiles over the castle walls as well as help to knock them down.

In this reconstruction of the siege of Jerusalem in 1187, invaders launch giant fireballs into the city.

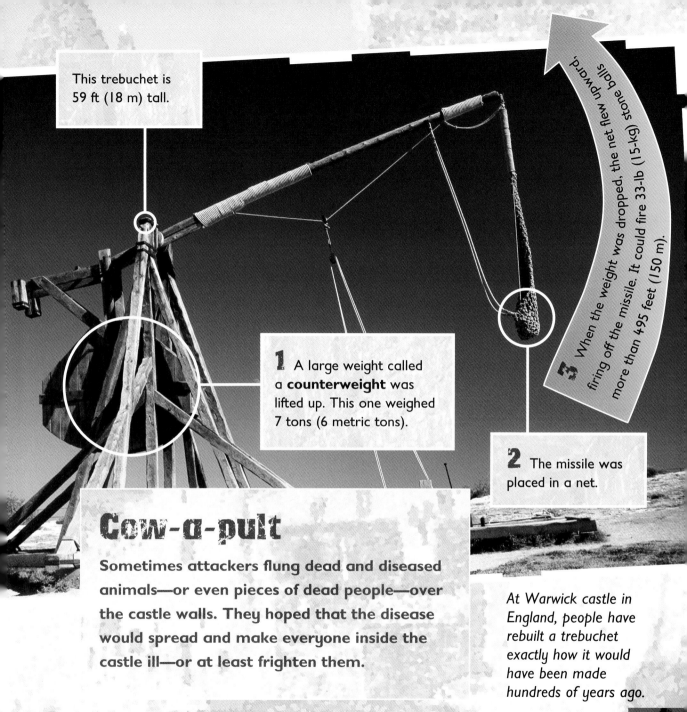

This trebuchet is 59 ft (18 m) tall.

3 When the weight was dropped, the net flew upward, firing off the missile. It could fire 33-lb (15-kg) stone balls more than 495 feet (150 m).

1 A large weight called a **counterweight** was lifted up. This one weighed 7 tons (6 metric tons).

2 The missile was placed in a net.

Cow-a-pult

Sometimes attackers flung dead and diseased animals—or even pieces of dead people—over the castle walls. They hoped that the disease would spread and make everyone inside the castle ill—or at least frighten them.

At Warwick castle in England, people have rebuilt a trebuchet exactly how it would have been made hundreds of years ago.

counterweight the large weight on the end of the trebuchet arm

Cannons and superguns

Using a mangonel or trebuchet was a good idea, but firing a giant stone ball at over 650 feet (200 meters) per second from a safe distance was even better.

When **gunpowder ignites**, the explosion contains far more energy than could ever be stored by stretching the strings of a crossbow. With **cannons**, it was much easier to bring a castle tumbling down.

Early cannons being fired at a castle. The soldier lighting the gunpowder stands well back.

Exploding cannon

The first cannons often misfired and injured the people firing them rather than the enemy. King James II of Scotland was killed by an exploding cannon.

ignites starts to burn

The world's first super-gun, the Great Turkish Bombard. It was first used in the 15th century.

The cannon uses the explosive energy from a chemical reaction to fire heavy cannonballs.

It could fire a stone ball of 660 lb (300 kg) …

… over 1 mile (1.6 km).

It could take over a week to get the bombard ready.

It needed several hundred men and more than 50 **oxen** to move it.

oxen   a special type of cow, bred for heavy pulling work

Castles still standing

It's amazing to think that some buildings made hundreds of years ago are still standing today—despite the attacks.

The castle has more than 50 towers.

Crenels for defenders to fire through

There are two circles of castle walls.

Carcassonne in southern France is an entire city inside a castle.

If attackers broke through the outer wall, they would be trapped by the inner wall.

A Martello tower was a simple castle or fort built in the 19th century, in some countries ruled by Britain. It was round so that soldiers could put a weapon on the roof and fire it in any direction.

Some castles were built for fun and not for defense. Belvedere Castle in Central Park, New York, was built in 1869.

Glossary

ballista large crossbow fired from a frame on the ground

battering ram large pole used to smash down castle walls

battlements narrow wall along the top of the castle wall to protect the castle's defenders

bolt short, heavy arrow fired from a crossbow

caltrops spikes used to slow down invaders by hurting their feet

cannon weapon using gunpowder that fires heavy balls a long way

catapult weapon used to throw an object a long way

counterweight the large weight on the end of the trebuchet arm

crenel (say "cre-nl") gap in the battlements for archers to fire arrows through

drawbridge bridge that can be raised and lowered to open and close the castle entrance

gravity the force that pulls all things downward

gunpowder mix of chemicals that explodes to fire weapons

ignites starts to burn

machicolation (say "match-ic-o-lay-shun") the overhanging part of the wall at the top of a castle. It has holes in it so that defenders can drop objects on enemy soldiers below

machine a piece of equipment with moving parts that does a particular job

merlon the solid part of the battlements for archers to hide behind

Middle Ages the time between the 5th and 15th centuries

missile any object thrown or fired toward a target

moat a huge ditch around a castle, usually filled with water

murder hole hole in the roof of the entrance to a castle used for dropping things on invading soldiers

oxen a special type of cow, bred for heavy pulling work

portcullis heavy metal or wooden gate used to open or close the entrance to the castle

pulley a wheel or set of wheels with ropes or chains. The ropes or chains are pulled over the wheels to lift or lower heavy objects.

siege tower (say "seej") tall tower that attacking soldiers used to try to break into a castle

treadwheel large wheel with a rope attached for lifting heavy objects. People walked inside the wheel to power it.

trebuchet (say "tre-boo-shay") weapon with a large weight attached, used for throwing heavy objects a long way

Further information

Books

Castle (DK Experience) by Richard Platt and David Nicolle (Dorling Kindersley, 2007)
Explores almost every aspect of life inside a castle in great detail.

Castles and Forts by Simon Adams (Kingfisher Publications, 2003)
A large-format book with lots of photographs covering the history of castles and forts from medieval times to more modern days.

I Wonder Why Castles Had Moats and Other Questions About Long Ago by Philip Steele (Kingfisher Books, 2004)
A large-format picture-based reference book that covers the key ideas along with interesting facts and information.

The Story of Castles by Lesley Sims (Usborne Publishing, 2004)
A story-based book with many illustrations, looking at the lives of those who lived in and around castles.

Usborne Little Book of Castles by Lesley Sims (Usborne Publishing, 2005)
A pocket-sized but wide-ranging guide with photos and illustrations.

Web sites

FactHound offers a safe, fun way to find Internet sites related to this book. All of the sites on FactHound have been researched by our staff.
Visit *www.facthound.com* for age-appropriate sites. You may browse subjects by clicking on letters, or by clicking on pictures and words.
FactHound will fetch the best sites for you!

Films

Robin Hood Prince of Thieves directed by Kevin Reynolds (Warner Brothers, 1991; PG rating)
An entertaining family adventure film looking at the life of the famous outlaw who lived in Sherwood Forest and battled against the evil Sheriff of Nottingham.

The Sword in the Stone directed by Wolfgang Reitherman (Buena Vista Pictures, 1963; U rating)
A Walt Disney retelling of the life of King Arthur, Merlin, and the Knights of Camelot.

Index